Ghost & *Other* Sonnets

GERALDINE MONK was born in Blackburn, Lancashire in 1952. Since first being published in the 1970s she has written six major collections of poetry and numerous chapbooks. Her writing has appeared extensively in the both the UK and the USA. As an extension to her activities in poetry she collaborates with many musicians including Martin Archer, Charlie Collins and Julie Tippetts. A collection of essays on her poetry, *The Salt Companion to Geraldine Monk*, edited by Scott Thurston, was brought out in 2007 by Salt Publishing.

Also by Geraldine Monk

POETRY
    Noctivagations (Sheffield: West House Books, 2001)
    Selected Poems (Cambridge: Salt 2003)
    Escafeld Hangings (Sheffield: West House Books, 2005)
    Raccoon (Boise: Free Poetry, 2007)

Ghost & *Other* Sonnets

GERALDINE MONK

CAMBRIDGE

PUBLISHED BY SALT PUBLISHING
14a High Street, Fulbourn, Cambridge CB21 5DH United Kingdom

All rights reserved

© Geraldine Monk, 2008, 2009

The right of Geraldine Monk to be identified as the
author of this work has been asserted by her in accordance
with Section 77 of the Copyright, Designs and Patents Act 1988.

This book is in copyright. Subject to statutory exception
and to provisions of relevant collective licensing agreements,
no reproduction of any part may take place without the written
permission of Salt Publishing.

Salt Publishing 2008

Printed and bound in the United Kingdom by Lightning Source UK Ltd

Typeset in Swift 9.5 / 13

*This book is sold subject to the conditions that it shall not,
by way of trade or otherwise, be lent, re-sold, hired out,
or otherwise circulated without the publisher's prior consent
in any form of binding or cover other than that in which
it is published and without a similar condition including this
condition being imposed on the subsequent purchaser.*

ISBN 978 1 84471 493 3 hardback
ISBN 978 1 84471 732 3 paperback

Salt Publishing Ltd gratefully acknowledges
the financial assistance of Arts Council England

1 3 5 7 9 8 6 4 2

For Lesley and David.

*My dear friends who
know the temperature of ghosts.*

Contents

GHOST

1	'It started with a tryst and twist of . . .'	3
2	'Light a nightlight flimsy . . .'	4
3	'Agitation shocked the public library . . .'	5
4	'Swallow-tail moth artificially lit . . .'	6
5	'Desperation clung to petulant . . .'	7
6	'Sided by accident she wandered in a . . .'	8
7	'Chronic webbings. Intrigue. . . .'	9
8	'The disembodied head looked . . .'	10
9	'Then another door shut in . . .'	11
10	'An unearthly grown so sickly he . . .'	12
11	'Newly installed double . . .'	13
12	'The trans-Pennine late night train . . .'	14
13	'An angularity of hate stoked the room . . .'	15
14	'Was it moving? In a heart . . .'	16
15	'Spell binder driven wet. Two . . .'	17
16	'Exaggeration of bird song impaled . . .'	18
17	'A cumulonimbus of cupped hands . . .'	19
18	'Bypassing that room no one dared . . .'	20
19	'Sciatica nerves slews posture . . .'	21
20	'Ghost of her ghosts . . .'	22

&

21	'In fear we lay longitudinal. . . .'	25
22	'The heart-shaped lavender was . . .'	26
23	'Parting such sweet succulent flesh . . .'	27
24	'She strained her eyes through muslin. . . .'	28
25	'A rare whiff. Aromas were way loud. . . .'	29
26	'Big-time snow deafened. Bedrooms . . .'	30
27	'Wasted suburban garden . . .'	31
28	'It recurs: the . . .'	32
29	'A second glance and then another . . .'	33
30	'When the fog partially cleared . . .'	34

31	'Not waking and finding herself...'	35
32	'Onto my frozen fingers came...'	36
33	'Driven to the edge by wind chimes...'	37
34	'So remote it was beyond...'	38
35	'Army of shadows infiltrates...'	39
36	'No cigarettes in the ashtray. Between a...'	40
37	'Topping the head...'	41
38	'Shocking pink lips kissed sepia...'	42
39	'What makes you look in at the...'	43
40	'In her heart of hearts larks and...'	44

OTHER

41	'Cornering on a black fen. From kerb to...'	47
42	'Something wicked this way...'	48
43	'Prising eyes against the future...'	49
44	'After three days with...'	50
45	'Batten down the letter box....'	51
46	'She slid one out. Delicately...'	52
47	'A distraught toe...'	53
48	'At the bottom of the bowl it nudged his...'	54
49	'What malice-driven hand...'	55
50	'Opening the envelope he found another...'	56
51	'When a storm sweeps up from...'	57
52	'For some reason it was in a...'	58
53	'Reconfiguring spaghetti...'	59
54	'Have I written this before? This...'	60
55	'Whatever it was it came to pass the...'	61
56	'Time out of mind the beasts of the pillows...'	62
57	'Stumpy staring in...'	63
58	'Water from the tap wasn't water...'	64
59	'Hefted sheep leap a burning moat. Mint...'	65
60	'Thus spake someone from the water...'	66
61	'Others floundered. Crashed awkward...'	67
62	'Swan song. Anticipation blitzed in a...'	68

'I stand in my absence in front of a thing
That stands in its presence and fits it
To perfection.'
—Peter Riley

Ghost

1

It started with a tryst and twist of
Lupine lovely arms along a rural railroad
Bank. Winter rose up summer's rise.
Throes of profound bafflement.
Vague was the impression of fossil
Teeth across the false breast
Yearning for a straight line in
Nature digging the *what* that lies
Oblong and lewd in the tube of
Afterlife lingerings.
Unsourced scent so strong it
Overpowered sense and narrative.

Disturbed earth grew stripes.
A stalk broke too far.

2

Light a nightlight flimsy.
Fingertip search. Distilled eye of owl.
Neck-head etched with chevron blaze.
Disconcerted ferns clutched
Breeze of little feet in lost cotton
Socks tripping hither came to
Pass a murthering stream concluding.
Happy-heart so young upon a
Devious pond to chance. Dragged by
Shady plankton mouth. Down-down.
Leery-long his slow green
Face replaced her woeful visage.

Egg-shaped love that shined up rooms.
For whom the gods love. Brut.

3

Agitation shocked the public library.
Pushes and scuffles nudged a thousand
Books—splendid to behold—into
Fits of hissy pulp. Parchments
Fell into silence please she passes
Disappointingly not white the *Grey Lady*
Glides gilded vellum lips. Hint of
Tongue. Authentic scrawls bemoan
Clingy narratives: her thwarted soul
Worries faux hieroglyphic
Codes dabbing Mille Flores on
Distressed temples. Perforated syntax.

A room much sadder for its off-white shade
Doomed to overwrite in perpetuity.

4

Swallow-tail moth artificially lit
Anglepoise. Alien apparent illumed.
Mandrake-shaped human catches exhale.
Midnight oily. Flying coppers buzz choppers
Riddle dull-rut backtrack. Blink of
Wing and lash. Shush. Electric
Standoff. Duel farce. Bluff of
Eyeballs. Mutually accusing dovetails.
Engrossment. *Aside*: Discarded kid
Gloves low-glow pearl buttons:
Bread in milk. Pobs. Feckless
Exposure. Unearthly whey. Sore-eye sight.

Almost day when they found them. Limpid
Heap of white & cream. Crumpled cold.

5

Desperation clung to petulant
Hillside. Sadistic clouds gingered
Nails snagged a cut of
Gibbous moon. It was getting nasty.
Eccentric crops of revert cats
Mewled semicircles beneath the bay
Window frocks shimmied in full party swing.
Transparency rebounded dark: looking
Out with awe they saw themselves looking
In: Thin things shattered on
Fluted reflections. As if . . .
They gasped . . . as if . . .

Grabbing the scruff a noun
Drowned an over-gowned thought.

6

Sided by accident she wandered in a
Shade knocking beamers off their
Brilliant yeah-day axis dimmed
Somewhat too sudden. Apprehensive
Frost evaporated certainty. Radiation of
Fossils things kindled underfoot. Couched
Blusters of embarrassments. You! You!
Blush driven guffaws nude metallic
Claws tendering raw unholy
Collision. Petrifaction happens. Not
Solely in the megalithic night but in the full
Bright of true and other yes.

Being scared stiff of shadows tires coloured
Balloons. Redesigns trusty schedules.

7

Chronic webbings. Intrigue.
Androgynous flush haunts
Reptilian spine vault gothic.
Vehement throb conflicts on
Polyphonic gutwire. Phantom strings
Berserk minor arpeggios. Buttress ups
Super star dome. Sanctuary out to lunch.
Alone and pale and sort of floaty
Fingers clutched the altar rails of dread
Draining the face with featureless
Caress a shaft of light carved through her
Strained glass prelude.

Fragmented fugues of spheres break
Wind on mobile ring tones. Discarnate.

8

The disembodied head looked
Browned-off. Crammed under an
Undeodorised pit: a pendulum
Seeps misshapen gore
Tenders X centuries O clock shadows.
Yonder staircase growing microbes
Gating post-world beings.
Heritage is a young word hung
Wearily around old corners. Shoulders
Peeve. Tempered daggers drawl.
Orion in ascendance belting three glee
Songs the eunuch clears high C.

Living things: better to be lost over heels than
Lose your head over love of detail.

9

Then another door shut in
Another room untouched by human
Hand they ate a late supper and
Smoked tubular fish ... dragging
Recalcitrant skeletons speculation
Hanged a cupboard full of nerves shredded
Gaunt. Vexed extremities gesturing
Haute couture of louche. Ruffled shirts
Clashed on décolleté *rather* risqué fault
Lines. Good-times. Tectonic
Harmonics trashing casements.
Supernatch coloratura *out-there* hair-raising.

Stopped in tracks. Seeing is not believing but
Retrieving fragments of deathly sweet wrappings.

10

An unearthly grown so sickly he
Died girlish young: translucence fixed in
Marble. In effigy without relief
Upon his death bed bound in medieval
Fug. Chapel-rot. The *Ship of Fools* sails
Upon the walls through none the wiser
Centuries receding. Spellbound with
Voyage she placed her palms upon his arms
Steadying her vertigo. Neck crane. Surge of
Flux. A tightening grasp of marble
Hand so slight the delicate light passed
Through its captive static: clasping hers in horror.

Sweetheart stoned in death. Please release her.
Let her go. Your tiny hand is frozen.

11

Newly installed double
Glazing did not block unnatural
Drops in temperature. Entering the
Bedroom quickshivers sheet down.
Neglected feet turn blue at the
Bottom of the embryonic bed the dying
Take refuge. Love-starved nature
Abhors a vacuum: it conjures bogus voices
Irks the kl-*tick*-kl-*tick* from the
Corner drawer where sulks of
Shirts and socks sleep
Softly   *softly*.

Rattle my mouth with dried black beans.
I show a bold face to your frosty throat.

12

The trans-Pennine late night train
Skirts thick sexy ankles: Mam Tor.
Kinder Scout. Sacred v secular. Head rut.
Peaks blether in marmite dark. Antlers
Caper. Campers and sheep snore sideways.
Blocking out carriage with iPod she
Flicked an irritated hair away up there a
Skein of lunar cycles stunts between
Tunnels. Phantom trolley cuts a cheesy gap.
Fallings out across the aisle. Toilets permanently
Engaged. Drunks snipe. Bicker bills. Moon
Coming full-on loud: stiff as synthetic ribbon.

Back home at last alone her mirror told the tale: a
Lunar globe right in middle of her forethought.

13

An angularity of hate stoked the room.
Glad dialogue posed. Bitter laps. Painted
Eyes followed everyone round and skin.
Almond. Feral furs. Sling-backs
Blew perfect teeth haphazard.
'Surfaces lightly values thickness'.
Waterish broth. Presumptive hunger after
Fame for what? At any cost his
Brag of genius reduced his
Thermometric liquid. On him alone the
Painted eyes spawned at dawn his
Self pawn within his fatal absolute.

Energy wasted in positioning posterity.
Apparent not real expansion of no body.

14

Was it moving? In a heart
Twitch the curtain sulked
Heavy with charge lay
Nap scarred beyond its fringe
A forlorn moan at altitude
Rafters cocked ears under eaves
Pierced with precision the
Looking glass shatters
Terror across the floor
Boards warp with viral
Wracking a ruinous sequence
Without a sound witness.

Confirmation in lament. The last
Wounded animal in the wood.

15

Spell binder driven wet. Two
Articles in start to finish trickle.
Unseen. Unfeel. Influence.
Unravelling feast: a beast
Engraved too light to trace.
(Oh Kathleen sing Willow Oh
Willow. Willow. Willow.)
Start to finish straggle two lying
Red-faced apples. Two names
Cut deep. Exaggerated
Fatally. Sunk. Sodden.
Uncredible weeping.

(Oh Kathleen sing Willow Oh
Willow. Willow. Willow.)

16

Exaggeration of bird song impaled
Confusion. Hotel room shrinks so.
Portuguese porcelain quivering
Fado. Blue glaze darkened a back street
Bar. Unpacking belongings: A string of pearls.
Gap-toothed comb. Sentimental cork. Forked
Lightning feathers a rod. Same old
Steeple un-same. Oddness displacing
Sky. Seagulls storm a spectacular.
Locals say they'd never seen the
Like. An older language surfaced. Whoa.
They packed their unbelongings. Quick.

When unbeknownst strikes—cuticles ridge.
Half-moons cowering. Opaque horror.

17

A cumulonimbus of cupped hands
Poised in plaster cast a strange
Hue. Carmine flowers sprouted
Nails. It was altogether too. She ran
From room to room poking all
Thumbs in her well amazed eyes: a fine
Line between a fine line multiplied
Teleplasmic crud stopping short a
Moment near bone. Sublime miss.
Where this was going she wasn't sure
Following. Objects objecting. Let
Them triumph their matter. She was outta here!

Not altogether crisp decisions hit the dust. The
Arrival of the Queen of Sheba heralded the washing up.

18

Bypassing that room no one dared
Sleep in. When was a never. Noises off
Wye—it quietly flowed a
Hundred miles or so away up
North she heard it down the phone.
Or was it love? Silence in translation
Misinterprets hush. Love aside
Bookish bloods curdled madly.
Wasteland space of vacant
Shelves occupied by real
Irrationals. Bilateral
Fiends sprig the yew tree.

Enhanced radiation. Mother of all
Confluences bred a plainchant vortex.

19

Sciatica nerves slew posture:
Empathic lightning thorns. A
Drubbing storm gets up. Temperature in
Flux: hot goes hotter when a sudden
Drop stills the cabin's ceiling leaks a
Mournful trickle: *the lark and the clear air*
Sad as a sad dog pawing the dead. Ships
Pass in the night. Wave. His face staring at
His face. Her face staring at hers. Each
Passenger waving at their doppelganger
Each not knowing which is for real.
Regression grows grim round the rushes.

Crux matters. Furiously funny women
Rendered humour to the bone. Men wept.

20

Ghost of her ghosts
Never left her waking
Days lengthened till the last sky
Lit her goodbye breeze. Lemurs on her
Back booed who goes where to
Follow. Ringed tails wrapped her
Final neck scarf-warm and ever
So pretty. It was a beautiful death.
Unclenched chiffon. Lily pond. Pity
She mumbled as her eyes opened
Wide with stiff-awake the next day.
Another bunch of now beginning. Again.

The garden had many failures.
Growing endearment takes its toll.

&

21

In fear we lay longitudinal.
Our exactitude with words
Drawn to cold old spaces quartered
Off the beaten tale. Others sobbed. A
Miniature robin's head flew into
Doll-syndrome. It was a trying time.
Bottlenecks of prophesies topping
Visions wasn't stiff British but
How the sun came up! Rugged
Cuisine lined our nervous eclipse.
The full-on-fry-up toasted shades
Wading through. Tracery of bombs.

Abandoned fragility. Human minds hurt
Some. Intelligent plastic splinters unmoved.

22

The heart-shaped lavender was
Lavender and heart-shaped.
In the light of this matter
The sudden drop in form
Into horns and a turned-up
Mouth blue upon a bitter chill
Across the sheet a rack of fingers
Creeped towards a cup of tea
Growing cold with a broken sixpence.
At the centre of the morning
Rushed an hour which time
Forgot to brush and still

No one knew the difference between
Gold and brown and golden brown.

23

Parting such sweet succulent flesh
Sorrows nest of fish bones. Tenderness
Wearily maternal. Touched. Three circular
Silent pies baked auto-da-fé: Heaven.
Earth. Underworld lay. Balanced. Acting.
Two pies absent joy. Multiples gather
Massacre. Out the blue. One man went to mow
Meadow blood. Budding blood. One man and
A woman went that day. Came. Mowed cold
Blood creation. Smug Gods. Glutton. Sacred shrugs
Uncouth. Vengeful shoulders. Martyrdom of
Crayons colouring yellowing suns. Charred grapes.

Nothing happens here but everything. All
Human life is *there-there* Petrushka.

24

She strained her eyes through muslin.
Obtuse vitreous slid. Inaccessible road.
Sodium-sick trucks gut a runnel of
Heavy comfort. She drew the gauze:
Pressing flesh on cold division
Palms, cheeks smudged a sweat of
Masterpieces down the beautiful sash. She:
Gorgeously monotype. Between impossible
Freedom mocking doors observed
Her kissable nape ran scars. Every
Boding step of stair feared next stark
Landing. Soiled face on yesterday's paper.

Unfeeling streets a refuge from home. A cry is a
Far cry beyond. Yonder orchids grow spittles.

25

A rare whiff. Aromas were way loud.
Pervasive cabbage hexed with seaweed.
Sixth sense on full alert. Real-time dread.
Frisson lacking source. Lax. Location of
Exit obscure. Fire a certain death doubles
Anxious feet running all night down unlit
Corridors. Fear-bolted stonework. Distressed dogs
Crushed with cage. Tidal bores out there
Ploughing five shifty gullies through the bay.
Fylde snakes swift a silent coasting brood.
Mussels. Salt-ridden swerves behind your back
Rising to the last mouth. Messages drown.

One morning in Morecambe. Breakfast chairs
Shrouded. Room empty. Rolling news. No eggs.

26

Big-time snow deafened. Bedrooms
Rimed with no heat. Freak freeze.
Gherkin bite. Inner cheek cringe. Mrs
Winter Jumps a galliard. Shovel up steamings of
Coddy muck. Down corned beef hash. Dog packs
Shape a stealth jet out the living daylights—
Last seen heading up Shakeshaft Street.
What year is this? Grunge atoms play tricks.
Skiffle. Pogo sticks. The beehived Queen of
Hearts weeps into a jar of jokes her back
Comb fashioned from a philosopher's bone.
Give up your chin to the buttercup sweet.

Kick long grass thought behaving badly.
Time snaps back in its bottle. Stopper fast.

27

Wasted suburban garden
Cut a deck of wolves through
Radio rap and barbeques
Playing flugelhorns with throaty
Spanish cards falling into packs of
Missing numbers.
Life as we know it in our
Glands lands a glancing blow.
We stop and listen hard to
Catch the drift of oceans in our
Pink-eared conch from a foreign
Sound as senses touch tip rim.

Aside from this we kiss the
Doldrums upping entropy to bliss.

28

It recurs: the
Black-gloved hand
Rude inside the front door
At four in the morning
Grappling to unhook the
Safety chain on Valentine's
Night. Animal yelp sent a
Bunch of fives miming
Syncopated scuttles
Down the frightened
Hallway spiders
Writhes.

Amid strewn hearts. Fond
Follies came a crop of reap.

29

A second glance and then another
Swift. Was it me or? Were my
Eyes in the back of my beyond-head
Reeling a bird-riff? I can't rightly
Remember never having called
Quits with beak. It did a flambé
Shim. Joy within the saucer flipped its
Own volition over. A rare day. So
This was spirit. Dunk away! Tasty
Dregs leave me wanting.
Tell me it's true what I saw in the
Doodle behind the drab.

Burnt toast. Spectaculars undreamt at
Breakfast. Blinds I drew. Ruffle-down riot.

30

When the fog partially cleared
Placing a sticky label on each
Eyelid seemed a droll idea. The
Night was longing. Arch and dirty
Dancing fermented lurid
Apparitions. Nameless acts with
Xmas hand lotion. Smudged lips redefining
Delicate matters. Disenchantment with
Beauty. Crude high-jinks. No age was
Innocence. Totemic banquet roosts and
Broods a freak-out. The out swoop was
Swift with low-down and shocking.

Banquo laughed to see such fun.
A snagged nail moves entrails.

31

Not waking and finding herself
Fabulous but needy on the kitchen floor
The bread-making machine had
Baked a skull. Typical. With each
Inversed incremental moon the
Stain on the wall behind the wall
Waxed and waxed and now this:
Brown bread!
Damned by death shaping the
Day ahead into inevitable uncertainty.
Sighing a wheat-field sough this
Clown of a loaf was the last straw.

She faded into backgrounds as all the
Rage around her grew. Some.

32

Onto my frozen fingers came
Unsolicited words. Laying a ghost
The design of our silent eyes we never—
Even our dreams being sheer snow
Shadows keep piling up surfaces to a
Higher level of appearance on the
Timepiece taxidermal. Ticker. Heart
Skips. Trapeze. Motion tracking
Sound. On light. Partly stone.
Partly the absence of stone. Trickery.
Surge of swirling limb defines the bandage.
Partly the absence of limb.

Who sent this terrifying beast
To hold my eyes absurdly stiffened with arc.

33

Driven to the edge by wind chimes
Some fleshy bits stick to the
Carving knife. Her father sighed
Pointy with war fatigue.
Induced atrocity euphoria.
Ephemeral drill. Distraction yells of
Bayonet practice. Attacking steak to
Tenderise the war bulletin on radio 5
Live 'It's rubbish' she cried. Unplayable
Grace notes pepper her throat.
Waves upon raids spat shock and
Cynical awe.

Biting the bullet she bought a German
Knife in Holland. Forgive her—Sheffield.

34

So remote it was beyond
God's back. So full-on-front
Marrow got a chance-child.
Oddity normal. Thumping big
Planets abounds. Jupiter a relative
Sprat. Let's not go there. Marvelling on
Radishes at sun rise. Wheelie bins. Red
Rubber bands dropped in a gleam by
Postmen: never the same one knocks:
Nothing is twice. Withered thespian
Mouth sprouting lurid tunes. Catapult of
Melodrama struts an aging stage. Plastered.

It's a being thing. Big hat villain dribbles
Moustache on baby. Grand piano mementos.

35

Army of shadows infiltrates
Late afternoon. Phew! What a
Scorcher. Butter-twist borders
Flag mirage. Patriotic uprights
Slouch. Big bellies out. Bum cracks. Hot
Haunches lumber. City slickers blotch
Blue-pit shirts. Arms sop under siege.
Buckles. Baby's shoes. Bachelor buttons. How
Many names in an English country garden grow:
Culverkeys. Two faces under one hat. Skullcaps.
Cains & Abels. Gogs & Magogs at
Noon other beings cross the room. Angel things.

Rub oil in overstretched palms. Global takes the
Hindmost. Hot potato—Cinderella?

36

No cigarettes in the ashtray. Between a
Mother and Patsy Cline lay crystal emptiness.
Ying. She accidentally wrote for *thing*.
Yang. Doubled-up flesh. Daughter. Furtive talk.
Imminent death parts the spectacular
Red Sea celluloid rushes. It's epic. Glass. As in.
Ashtray shrugs resplendently unused
Splits its self asunder. Clean in two
Dying emotions. Half-mooned. Mother broke
First. ((Things happened around her)).
Upstairs. Daughter's old bedroom door
Banged everly on that total windless night.

Simple protest stultifies the complex.
Too much protestation — the telephone rang.

37

Topping the head
Heights begat a dropping
Down-z-round Snake Pass. A city.
A lit distant horizontal plain as
Daylight playing suntricks
Beyond the peaks and
Dark waters whiter than a
Southern Spanish town it
Shone a hover outing
Heavy reddish bricks
Residually hacking-soot.
Fact to face with wonder.

Three needless dead the night before
Morning. Manchester in a state of vision.

38

Shocking pink lips kissed sepia
Photo. Flaky pastry shatters
Mouths spread-eagled on her lap.
Medals of war drop jawless. Clam
Grief. Limpet cling. Delicious was the
Weepings at weddings. The self-playing
Guitar strums desolation so low down
Ears depress. Scalps peppermint. Shocking
Pink lips kissed sepia photograph. Flaky
Pastry shatters clipped mouths
On her lap. Saturated fat. Medals tinkle.
Chocolate buttons. Home fires. Tinned postcards.

Gaping space frames bereavement. Unoccupied
Armchairs. Demolishment of territories.

39

What makes you look in at the
Exact window where someone is
Looking out? Inexplicable encounters
Traduce unknowns with wary
Other. What is behind that sticky girl one
Step stunningly away from heaven? Tossed.
A thing of beauty in a room so ordinary.
Mindless kicks. Burns. Bite hard words
Mocking back-broke loveliness. Ape
Ghosts. Rapes-ghosts reel on little
One. Well below a Restoration rake-hell
Humans shouldn't figure. Let alone . . . let alone . . .

Neglected screams in a field of unwashed forks.
Far crying buried in gust of shush-love.

40

In her heart of hearts larks and
Exultations tired her heavy
Good. Robbed. Her precious soul
Hung out to dry—love left the
World as she knew it. Tucks of
Emotional ocean killed by root
Equations. Long in tooth fabled
Beasts lined up to haunt her sunken
Hinterland. Overcast. Punctuated. O.
Reek of exist. Unnourished skin gorged
Its own barrier. Floodgates seeped
Double deadly wet stuff. Lust for absence.

Wished upon a bone. Broken wonderland.
Ruptured dreams. Beloved. Broken amour.

Other

41

Cornering on a black fen. From kerb to
Eternity. Cold-war-winter-bicker. Atomic
Landscape. Belly yawl. On top of this
Fathoming where the ship listed turned
Knuckles to absence. Improbable figments
Coughed clear bronchial fronds. Fibrous
Weft dislodged bits of lung. Skin dust flecked.
Eyes shed buckets. Spectres fool play. I
Pinched my mind set. Me-speak. Recovery
Came slow beneath the floating of Ely a
Circle of angels spun a honey trap. My last
Thoughts remaindered.

All at sea once more.
Maroon will never be the new black.

42

Something wicked this way
Turned a ruptured face up the
Downs the devil himself trilled a
Gash cutting Sussex in two
White heads sway a floral after-mauve.
Awol mare on all fours bolts the car
Inching death within a tease of
Wild-side. Hooves rear mazed.
Strawberry roan swags a blaze of
Dreamt-on couchant. A feather from where
Ever balanced motionless on the steering
Wheel: Veering on invitation.

Stuff happens. Getting interpersonal
With death sheers the flocking wallpaper.

43

Prising eyes against the future:
Vermillion it was. Very venison blood.
The semi-derelict house was now all hers.
Depressed furniture. Curtainless. Fridge
Bare. Life boxed up. Scuppered dreams.
Naked bulbs. Unpacked shades. Doomy
Exhaustion. Powder mouth. Pot noodle. Doubts
Reformed. Big mistake. Vague was the touch
Upon the elbow. Violent the emotion. Harps
Hung from willows. Rings crossed. Mice
Turned turtle. Insects grew hoofs. Treacle of bees in
The night. Devoid bred voids behind voids. Din dark.

Nothing was like like. Lashings of
Metaphors confounded mad god logic.

44

After three days with
Bits of sea between her
Teeth a wounded knee
Widowed her hair. Strafed with
Newly weeds and something borrowed on
The beach strewn a ghastly flotsam. Galactic
Children skrieked with melting under
Donkey hides darkening pleasure
Belly-up on the blinding
Out-of-tune piano.
Foreign as they come out the blue-crashing
Light played the brindled limbs.

Who on earth was what and after
Which life roosted death?

45

Batten down the letter box.
It drifts its upper lip in an up-wind.
Snaps down demand. We
Answer the front door whimsy
To Nobody over and
O-signs of ghastly joining
Together our faces with
Something other than love
Gasps if a fleshed-out
Shape blocks the
Opposite. Opposite.
Wall cushioning a flash of scud.

Seeing nobody in repeat tires the heart:
Out-fears the stranger stranger.

46

She slid one out. Delicately.
Thumb high tabernacles on the
Brink. Segs of life in niches. Miniature
Scent bottles. Eyelash in aspic. A sweet
Rootless milk tooth. Rare bird shell.
Scale of a Killamarsh great crested newt
Exquisiting in finial caprice.
Immaculate juice suspending
Essence. Anointed fragments
Falling remorselessly towards
Stone floor disillusionment. World
Shattered to dread and curious silence.

He slid one out. Delicately. Another
Shattered to dread and curious silence.

47

A distraught toe
Falters on the cast-iron
Frog. Stop. Right there. Organic bruise
Spreads motley-puce beyond the ankle
Crushed ice on thin skin.
Oh wonderworld!
Your hungry maw perfects your oyster.
Pearl-perfect blotting the harsh-edge
Rows over-bright blood cruising
Keenness to the quick.
Perverse inanimates ride high on exhaustion.
Hidden mood-runners shoot reality.

Speculation is rife:
Life is a glorious loophole.

48

At the bottom of the bowl it nudged his
Hand. Lurking unnameable from where and
What or why but never had he seen. In a
State controlling nervous system he tried not to
Vomit. Longhand slouched to backhand
Writing his goodbye note upon a
Paper bag. *What aberration under heaven*
On earth touched me he scrawled and
Spiked it on a cup hook. Hanging presence
From a tree baffled crowds cowered a shock.
His makeshift horns and forked tail
Clashed in the sun fierce with unrelenting.

Life takes root in such a simple culture.
Smocked-ones throwing turnips at a witch.

49

What malice-driven hand
Shaped these nightshade words? Cram
Fisted. Rasps of ingle spite. Snooks
Cocked slicing clean through
Solids. Seeking pointed solace she
Withdrew under the table screwed
Courage to a ball binned with furious
Riddance. Job done. As day yawned
Her drawn face slept on through
Regrouping words appalling. Cornering
Eyelids. Slithering the iris. Trickle through pupils.
Entering in: Sliding south towards her heart.

Words unfurled. Fin things swam
Backwards. Vegetation uprooted their spots.

50

Opening the envelope he found another
Ad absurdum. Zilch-sized peeled to
Microbe then all those pesky angels on
A pin head fell onto his crotch: The answer is
Two thousand and one. He woke and
Breathed relieved his situation normal:
Except his bed was in the wrong
Place facing an impossible wall and
Way over the dressing table he had to
Crawl to reach the door blocked by a
Blasted oak wardrobe. Severed wooden
Legs baulked his exit. Unremarkable room
Saturated with situation.

Porous dreams distress the linen.
Nodes grow discordant rearrangements.

51

When a storm sweeps up from
Ringinglow spirits lour. Serious
Migraines lose identity. Thick
Temples pulsate. Torrential mutability.
Gabble Ratchets ride roughshod
Intortus. Harbingers of doom
Coming to take you away. Welter of
Seers finger wag. Beloveds hug tight.
Not now. Not tonight. Manoeuvres
Tulip. Wicks bit to elbows. Glow-in-the-dark
Lunar calendar falls from wall trashing a
Year of moons. It was messy.

Barnacle Geese reclassified as fish or fruit
Eaten under the subterfuge of natural language.

52

'FOR SOME REASON *it was in a*
Pink shampoo bottle' croaked the
Radio. This sentence curled the
Paper where her toe nails fell in
Furls: bathroom tiles convulsed
Plasmatic. *'The hand pouring*
It was grimy.' Sluice that gormish
Tongue. All tomorrows bolted up her
Backboned larynx. Notes froze her
Little fingers: Scallions a dangle.
Throat of ganglions
Sprung taut. Umber of lauds.

Sing everybody sing *because we are cheerful.*
Music scares the ghost and occupies the preface.

53

Reconfiguring spaghetti
Hoops the child-weary child
Redefined joy. On the peninsular a
Narked wind got up a torment of
Choughs. Red legs and bills snap
Dragon. The art deco tower inclining
Towards gothic was afire. Weird.
Home hills twist a menace. Petrified
Eyes at every heart lurch of bend.
Free-wheeling crustaceans
Below sea level sang: *'Little mercies'*
Phantom crabs of the Isle of Man trill descant.

Twist another face of deck pips spreading
Two-faced cards across a clothless table.

54

Have I written this before? This
Moment reoccurring. Translating the
Space between signs backs up collision.
I try again. Slabs break nuance. Have
I written this before? I'm not getting beyond
The first page endlessly. June. 1.02 a.m.
Weather warnings. Flood alerts. Cities vie for
Bright. Height. Dazzle. Layers of apartment blocks
Block traces. Tectonic plates binge hyper. Earth
Restless. Reclaiming. Slabs break finesse.
Have I written this before another dawn?
Grubby robes of memory bake obscure placement.

This instance miniscules out its kilter.
Still falls the rain. Still falls the rain.

55

Whatever it was it came to pass the
Third person in-fronting a face-off.
Tics fed off stunted dialogue. The ayes
Have it. The nose delinquent. We can't go on
Bleating like this. Rude life sows
Affronted oats in winds. Connected
Cells simper all night in the dell of desperate
Proximity. Unspeakable awareness of
Genitalia at funerals. Immodest
Proposals. Vexed communions with the
Very dead proliferates with dry sherry.
On a late night bus a shoddy jacket scries.

Sea a long way away. Shrimp-things called.
Proffer a disheartened cheek to a no-kiss. Gentle-so.

56

Time out of mind the beasts of the pillows
Lolled. The love of ceilings: Untouchable.
Intimate. Infinite. Hairline cracks. Incipient
Webs. If it should fall. Oh god if it should
Meet the face. *Bin that thought.* Tail that
Headlight—*at this time of night?* Scent its
flight. Oh. It's gone. Kingfishers. Do you
Love kingfishers? Look. It's there! Oh. It's
Gone. Was I the only one who thought I'd
Seen that shooting star. There are as many
Rainbows as observers. Look! A glorious
Display of multifaceted aloneness. Oops. Gone.

Swan-necking is not a form of kiss
Just checking out that we exist.

57

Stumpy staring in:
A mad thing. Peeping tomb.
Bowels churn a
Contort of heather roots.
Extreme appearance rating
Replicating meat. A cart of bruise
Upsets rotting fruit. Mildew
Fret. Trench foot. Blacker than
Black fly. Aye. God's teeth tearing up the
Belly of a pristine path thickened with
Gangrene so ripe it hurt the edgeless
Regions of soul. Lock all doors. Windows.

Worry beads sown and grown anew.
Sup a froth and blend with after-road kill.

58

Water from the tap wasn't water.
Faces emerged from soap. Cuffs scum.
Denying nothing soused doubt.
Saxa salt brags *no need to grind* at
Four in the morning. Is that necessary?
Green madrigals tease deserts.
O Cecilia swimming in dimmer lights.
Let there be late! Being early for owls is gracious.
Longed sleep we forego. Del Monte pears
Illume the darkest war days. Straw
Buffers tins. Cardboard box and a battered
Violin hangs loose with the Sacred Heart.

Remembrance of things wafer. Fins. Scales.
Another time more vivid. Out of this world.

59

Hefted sheep leap a burning moat. Mint
Little lungs maul the idyll baa.
Pastoral collapse. Umbles of earth drape
Space. Lost in big. Universal
Striped pyjamas: old sleep-sweat
Greets glory morning. Citrus squirt.
Eyes hurt. Basilica blue. For three long days
Nuts have lain. Forlorn. Assimilation
Begging. Wild life cat strike. Finches.
Squirrels. The whole motley etcetera of
Mobiles in absentia. Slanting days to sotto.
Brilliance off key. Wind moves little.

When gardens fall quiet
Conundrum barks a foul magic.

60

Thus spake someone from the water
Boiler. Manish. Transonic. Curdled
Arias mutate. Polyphonic cockerel
Crows. Necked hens. Womanish. Rhapsodic
Wands. Amidst all this her name came. God
Again? Blankets screwed in little lobes: *'Shall
We shell thee—shy podded pea? Shall we?'*
Crammed cloth and other textiles. Ears
Pearl. Her bed a boat. Dressing table floats.
Teeth lisp. Frivolous liquid in sinister bottles.
Attic door opening. To see the moon. Attic door
Opening. To see the moon—stand on a chair.

Green minds overhang gables. End terraces
Ramblings unchecked. Put your leg in bed.

61

Others floundered. Crashed awkward.
Awkward states of random corruption.
Worrying beads to extinction. Starving
Tenderness. A branch of spurious truces
Stacked cards to the brink. Struggled on
Loveless. Witless. Dragged ghostly
Atmospheres round. Around. Sucked.
Succulence bemused. Removed. Be
Moved. Grew trivia. Fed rivalry with
Banners. Banned movement. Played with
Playback. Bewildered with commotion.
Day as grey as grey suits.

The gathering of spirits at crossroads bedevils
Surveillance. Incorruptible extravagance blocks envy.

62

Swan song. Anticipation blitzed in a
Wink. Resisting oblivion. Blind bulbs.
Swaddled love gifting cauliflower florets.
Stem cells cower. Sting jet tags cyclone
Genesis. Alpha storm. Pit of plover skins
Snuggle. Butter fingers. Comfort custard. Fight
To lick the bowl. Who dares go first on the
Dance floor. Trance. Apocalypse
Wow. Hosts of leavened gussets. Fig
Biscuits for breakfast. Sultry fruit. Beautiful
Fools we. Our thoughts gazelle
Yonder out our ape frames. Just another day.

Strange ones this token is for you.
If you've danced with me you must be true.

Acknowledgements

The Reality Street Book of Sonnets, *Stimulus Respond*, *Signals: Poetry Magazine*. Also a very special thank you to Jeff Hilson.

www.ingramcontent.com/pod-product-compliance
Lightning Source LLC
LaVergne TN
LVHW041345080426
835512LV00006B/621